The Faces of Gettysburg

The Faces of Gettysburg

Photographs from the
Gettysburg National Military Park Library

Edited by
JoAnna M. McDonald

Rank and File Publications
1926 South Pacific Coast Highway Suite 228
Redondo Beach, California 90277

1997

ISBN Number 1-888967-00-5
Library of Congress Catalog Number 97-069518

First Edition

Printed on acid-free recycled paper in the United States of America
Cover design by Ken Hammond

Dedication:

To Michael B. Hardy

"The Eyes are the Window to the Soul."

--DuBartes, circa 1590

Additional Titles Available from
Rank and File Publications

A Day With Mr. Lincoln: Essays Commemorating the Lincoln Exhibition at the Huntington Library
Edited by Richard Rollins

Blue and Gray Laughing: A Collection of Civil War Soldier's Humor
Edited by Paul Zall

Black Southerners in Gray: Essays on Afro-Americans in Confederate Armies
Edited by Richard Rollins

"The Damned Red Flags of the Rebellion": The Confederate Battle Flag at Gettysburg
By Richard Rollins

"Double Canister at Ten Yards": The Federal Artillery and the Repulse of Pickett's Charge
By David Shultz

Guide to Pennsylvania Troops at Gettysburg
By Richard Rollins and David Shultz

Pickett's Charge: Eyewitness Accounts
Edited by Richard Rollins

The Returned Battle Flags
Edited by Richard Rollins

Table of Contents

Preface

An interesting visit to the Gettysburg battlefield begins at the Visitor Center, with a close look at the Wall of Faces. The Gettysburg National Military Park has mounted a fascinating group of photographs from its Library. In 8" x 10" format, it is an awe-inspiring display, giving us an opportunity to look directly into the eyes of the men who fought and died in the battle. If we pause and look closely, we can begin to see them as individual human beings not much different than you and I. They were ordinary American citizens from all walks of life who found themselves in extraordinary circumstances. Most had families who missed them; many also had temporarily given up school or work to follow the flag of their company or regiment. These photographs put a human face on the words and actions we read and write about in our books.

I have always loved picture books, especially those about the men who fought the war. As a child I was perhaps the only person in my hometown who frequently borrowed *Miller's Photographic History of the Civil War* from the Carnegie Public Library. I studied the photographs for hours and memorized the poetry which so richly illustrated their experiences and narrated their adventures.

Yes, *adventures*. The majority of Civil War volunteers were in their teens and twenties when they signed up early in the war. The Civil War was the great adventure of their generation and the enthusiastic and energetic young men from all parts of the country portrayed on the Wall of Faces sought to become part of it. Photographs helped them remember and document their transition from civilian to soldier, recording what they did and how they looked. The little pieces of tin or paper were sent home to wives, mothers and sweethearts.

It is tempting to look at the images of Civil War soldiers and think that their lives were easy and simple. Most were rural people, used to the work habits of the farm and small town. Many had never left home, and the army offered an opportunity to see the country.

Yet the reality of their experiences during the war often turned out to be quite different from what they expected. Life in camp was tedious; combat, often deadly. They saw friends and neighbors torn to shreds in front of them, or dying from a strange disease.

Soldiers often formed strong friendships among themselves that lasted the rest of their lives, and even developed respect for their enemies. People at home, especially in the North, continued their lives with considerably less stress, often uncomplicated by the whipsaw of national events. By 1865 many volunteers wanted only to go home and resume their lives. Their war weariness resulted in fewer photographs being taken toward the end of the war.

After the war the kind of photograph collected in this volume became very unpopular: men tended to forget their experiences in combat. When veterans began organizing about 20 years later, they rediscovered photographs that they had hidden away in drawers and closets. More than one old soldier had his picture taken in his uniform in the 1880s and 90s, but we have not included those.

In recent years remarkable research by collectors and authors such as William Frassanito in *Gettysburg: A Journey in Time* and *Early Photography at Gettysburg,* and Greg Mast, in *State Troops and Volunteers: A Photographic Record of North Carolina's Civil War Soldiers,* have produced fascinating results bearing insights into the lives of Civil War soldiers. They have taught us to look at Civil War photos with different eyes. We now examine them closely to see what clothes the men wore and what weapons they carried; who they went to war with (and with whom they chose to have their pictures taken); the battles they fought, their wounds and how they were cared for. They can also tell us much about the nature of their deaths.

This book of photographs is not based on the same type of research. Yet patterns do appear, and several of the photos reveal important human connections. Civil War soldiers shared their experiences with fathers, brothers, cousins, and other men from their neighborhood, town and state. When they went off to fight, they often did so as families or as companies raised in their local area. This fact shaped all of their experiences, including how they fought.

It is our good fortune that the technology that produced these photographs required a length of exposure that forced the subject to stand still while posing. Tintypes were durable, an end product, not negatives and thus could be made instantaneously. Paper prints made from negatives, called Carte-de-Visites, were traded and used as calling cards.

Many of the photographs included here were taken early in the war, before the carnage of Bull Run, Fredericksburg and Gettysburg. Photographs of Federal troops are far more common than Confederates. The Northern blockade of Southern ports cut off chemicals that were needed to produce them. By 1863, silver compound, bromide, silver chloride and other chemicals became almost not-existent in the South.

All of the photographs in this book are in the Gettysburg National Military Park Library. Since the 1930s park historians and rangers have collected copies of photographs as well as letters, diaries, reminiscences, regimental histories and other documents written by the soldiers. Many have been donated by descendants while others were copied by hand or as typescripts by various individuals. They have over 500 photographs, and the number grows each year.

Gettysburg historians have benefited greatly from the collection of manuscripts and books in the Gettysburg National Military Park Library. It is a moving experience to pull out a letter such as the one written by Alexander Webb, commander of the brigade of Union troops who defended the Angle against the onslaught of the Confederate tide on July 3rd, in which he described his experiences. The original is in the Yale University Library in New Haven, Connecticut, but the park has a photocopy. In the Gettysburg Library I first saw the letter written by Capt. Henry Owen, 18th Virginia, describing the moment he watched the flank attack by Stannard's Vermont Brigade during Pickett's Charge. It was included in *Pickett's Charge: Eyewitness Accounts*. The photograph included here was also in the files. Both were donated by descendants. On the Wall of Faces I first saw the photograph of Pvt. Marshall Sherman, 1st Minnesota, with the flag of the 28th Virginia he captured on July 3rd. I learned that the 28th's flag is still in the Minnesota Historical Society and conveyed that information to The Museum of the Confederacy. They in turn had the color photograph made of it that appeared in their 1995 exhibition on Pickett's Charge. The same photograph is published for the first time in *"The Damned Red Flags of the Rebellion": The Confederate Battle Flag at Gettysburg*.

The importance of the extraordinary collection in the Gettysburg National Military Park Library can-not be overemphasized. It will get even better in the future, for many more photographs, letters, diaries and reminiscences written by soldiers and veterans lie hidden in state, local and county libraries all over the country. Any publisher's profits from this book will be used to help collect that information and donate it to the Library, thus making it available to future generations seeking to understand the men and the largest battle of America's bloodiest war.

An objective of the editor and publisher of this volume is to print the photographs as large and as clear as possible. In the best of all possible worlds, each photograph would be 8" x 10" Thus the captions are restricted to three lines and are drawn from the material in the files. The photographs are presented as the battle developed, beginning with those who participated in the events of July 1st. They are also in alphabetical order within each day. A few are out of sequence: horizontal photographs are placed at the end of a section and George, John and William Dabney Stuart are placed so that the brothers could be together. We have chosen as many as possible from the "rank and file" with the assumption that photographs of their officers, and especially the prominent generals, are widely available elsewhere. Those faces are familiar; ours are virtually unseen.

The photographs collected here have been waiting for many years for someone to print them together. It took the energy, intelligence and skill of JoAnna McDonald to get the job done. Her ability with a camera is evident; without her knowledge and enthusiasm this book would not exist.

Richard Rollins
Redondo Beach, California
Labor Day, 1997

Introduction:
Gettysburg's Wall of Faces

In the 1500s Leonardo da Vinci invented the first crude camera. Through the years many significant changes occurred in photography. By the 1800s a new, inexpensive process of developing photographs was invented. The cameramen called it wet-plate photography. Instead of using expensive glass plates, the photographers utilized tin plates, "tintypes." In turn, inexpensive paper prints could be made from these tintypes.

When the Civil War broke out thousands of amateur soldiers, dressed in their new, clean uniforms, posed for the photographer. Entire families sat for the photographer in order to obtain a visual record of the moment—to remember the face of their beloved father, son, brother or husband. They knew their loved one could die of disease in camp or be killed on some distant field. In turn, soldiers carried photographs with them to keep a part of home near their side. For thousands of war-torn families the photograph became the object which bound them together. Dr. Oliver Wendell Holmes, from Massachusetts, described photographs as "the social currency, the sentimental greenbacks of civilization."

When entering the display area of the Visitor Center at the Gettysburg National Military Park in Gettysburg, Pennsylvania, one will see a wall of photographs of individuals who fought in that famous battle over one hundred years ago—July 1, 2, and 3, 1863. This exhibit is known as the Wall of Faces and was established around 1987. The images represent only a small number of the Union and Confederate soldiers who participated in the battle. By viewing the exhibit the visitor is introduced to these men, thereby reducing the staggering numbers to individual personalities. To their relatives and friends these soldiers were not just numbers and statistics; they were fathers, brothers, husbands and lovers. The wall includes those who were killed or wounded in the battle and those who survived.

Gettysburg has received many images from private collectors and family members—to date, over five hundred photographs fill their files. The exhibit ensures that the images and human legacy of our ancestors is not lost to future generations. For example,

with the donation relatives often include an interesting anecdote. A soldier in the 1st Minnesota is pictured with a captured battle flag. A Vermont cavalryman left his wounded horse at Gettysburg, but the faithful animal, named "Abe," followed the unit and caught up with his master at Hagerstown, Maryland about sixty miles from Gettysburg.

Because there is not enough room to display all five hundred photographs a rotation system has been instituted. Approximately fifty photos are on display for about three years at a time. This system may change, however, as there are plans to expand the exhibit and lengthen the tenure of each image.

This album displays 200 of those men who were wounded, died or survived unscathed in the largest battle ever recorded in American military history—the Battle of Gettysburg.

The book is divided into three parts, July 1, 2 and 3. Within each section the photographs are organized in alphabetical order for the convenience of the reader. All ages herein are the approximate age of the individual during the time of the battle.

With the cooperation of the Gettysburg National Military Park this book goes one step further and allows patrons to take home with them a piece of America's history, to keep these soldiers' memories and faces alive. If you would like information on how to donate a photograph of a soldier who fought at Gettysburg please write to:

Wall of Faces Coordinator
Gettysburg National Military Park
97 Taneytown Road
Gettysburg, PA 17325

I would like to thank my family—Barbara and Norman McDonald, Elizabeth and Rebecca, my friend Mike Hardy and all my other friends for their support.

Much thanks go to D. Scott Hartwig, chief ranger at the Gettysburg National Military Park, Troy Harman, Director of the Wall of Faces, Darrell Smoker, the Gettysburg National Military Park librarian, and the entire staff at the National Park for allowing me to reproduce many of their photographs. David Shultz submitted interesting facts for several of the individuals.

This project, however, could not have been accomplished without the cooperation of hundreds of individuals, several historical societies, and other institutions who donated images to the Gettysburg National Military Park. A list of donators is included in the photo-bibliography.

JoAnna M. McDonald
Labor Day, 1997

Pvt. M. Hezekiah Allen, Co. H, 13th Alabama
Wounded and captured near Herbst's Woods,
exchanged November, 1863.

Pvt. George H. Atkins, Age 22
Co. D, 84th New York, killed.

Capt. G. T. Baskerville
Co. I, 23rd North Carolina, killed in Forney's field,
near Oak Hill and Oak Ridge.

Pvt. Charles E. Beard, Co. I, 33rd Massachusetts
Barely escaped a leg wound when a bullet hit his
canteen.

Pvt. Phillip Bennetts, Age 21
Co. F, 7th Wisconsin.
Wounded, died July 4, 1863.

Pvt. Peter Boyer, Age 20
Co. C, 17th Pennsylvania Cavalry
Helped hold back the Confederates north of town.

Pvt. George Brodmerkel (seated)
Co. B, 7th Wisconsin
Wound in the right breast, survived.

Cpl. James Brown
Company B, 97th New York
Killed.

Col. Henry Burgwyn, Age 20
26th North Carolina, killed.

Lt. John Calef
2nd U.S. Artillery, Battery A Horse Artillery
Positioned six guns on McPherson's Ridge, survived.

Pvt. Chester Cammer
Co., K, 142nd Pennsylvania, wounded and captured.

2nd Lt. Benjamin F. Carr
2nd Maine Arty, Battery B. Replaced Calef's guns on
McPherson's Ridge. Survived.

Sgt. Jefferson Coates, Co. H, 7th Wisconsin
Blinded during the battle, awarded a Medal of Honor
for gallantry.

Pvt. William H. Connell
Co. B, 149th Pennsylvania, wounded and captured.

Pvt. Charles Cosgrave, Age 22.
Co. D, 134th New York. Emigrated to the U.S. from
Ireland, 1854. Killed in action north of town.

Maj. Edward Croft, 14th South Carolina
Wounded and captured.

Capt. Simeon B. David, Co. A, 14th Georgia
Survived; killed at the Wilderness, May 5, 1864.

Pvt. Frank H. Elvidge
Co. A, 150th Pennsylvania
Captured and imprisoned in Richmond.

Lt. J. R. Emerson, Co. E, 26th North Carolina
Wounded, left on the field for dead, later died from
wounds.

Pvt. Edward Field, Age 20
Co. B, 13th Massachusetts
Shot in left lung, died July 2 or 3.

Pvt. Joseph Haas, 150th Pennsylvania
Teamster at Maj. Gen. Abner Doubleday's HQ;
wounded at the Wilderness, May, 1864.

Capt. James A. Hall, 2nd Maine Lt. Arty., Batt. B
Deployed his guns just south of the railroad cut near
McPherson's Ridge; survived.

Cpl. Franklin N. Halsey
Co. F, 147th New York; killed.

Pvt. John T. Handy, Co. F, 52nd North Carolina
Fought July 1 and 3; survived.

Lt. William Harris, Co. F, 45th North Carolina
Killed.

Pvt. Jacob Hershberger
Co. C, 142nd Pennsylvania; survived.

Sgt. Amos Humiston, Age 32
Co. C, 154th New York. Killed, found clutching a
photograph of his three children..

Pvt. William (L) and Sgt. Charles (R) Issermoyer
Co. D, 153rd Pennsylvania
William was captured, both survived.

Capt. Jacob Jacobs, Co. F, 83rd New York
Wounded, survived.

Pvt. Alex Lameraux, Co. D, 143rd Pennsylvania
Captured, died in prison, October, 1863.

Pvt. Charles E. Leland, Age 18
Co. B, 13th Massachusetts
Shot in the lower abdomen, killed.

Cpl. Henry A. Miller, Co. G, 26th Wisconsin
Survived

Cpl. Benjamin McPherson
Co. E, 149th Pennsylvania
Killed.

Capt. Daniel Marston, Co. C, 16th Maine
Survived.

Cpl. James Martindale, Age 24
Co. E, 26th North Carolina
Wounded in the chest, survived and died in 1918.

Pvt. Michael McGurren, Co. G, 97th New York
Survived the battle and the war. Became a legal
citizen in 1892.

Pvt. John Moy, Age 25, Co. H, 6th Wisconsin
Survived assault on Railroad Cut, killed in battle of
Spotsylvania, May, 1864.

Pvt. George F. Newton, Age 22, Co. C, 61st Georgia
Wounded in the left elbow and captured. Union
surgeons amputated his arm, but he survived.

Pvt. Issac P. Nichols, Age 23
Co. E, 134th New York. Survived.

Sgt. Robert Niven, C. H, 8th New York Cavalry
Survived.

Sgt. John H. Peifer, Co. E, 17th Pennsylvania Cavalry
Supported Calef's battery near Chambersburg Pike;
survived.

Pvt. Valentine Painter
Co. G, 151st Pennsylvania
Wounded in the forehead, survived, died in 1905.

Pvt. William H. Porter
Co. E, 142nd Pennsylvania
Survived.

Capt. John D. H. Robinson, Co. F, 13th Alabama
Survived.

Pvt. Jeremiah Royer
Co. L, 17th Pennsylvania Cavalry, survived.

Col. William Sackett, 9th New York Cavalry
Deployed his regiment north of the Chambersburg
Pike. Mortally wounded in 1864 in Virginia.

Pvt. Thomas C. Sheppard, 1st South Carolina
Killed.

Lt. John J. Smith, Age 21, Co. H, 80th New York
Fought near McPherson's Ridge and survived.

Pvt. William F. Smith, Co. H, 2nd Mississippi
Killed.

Pvt. Edward Sonneberg, Age 42
1st N.Y. Light Artillery, Battery I
Fought on Cemetery Hill; wounded and killed.

Pvt. Benjamin L. Taylor , Co. F, 26th North Carolina
Slightly wounded in left heel. His company sustained
100% casualties.

Lt. John F. Tinker, Age 23
Co. K, 84th New York
Survived.

Lt. Morton Tower, Co. B, 13th Massachusetts
Captured, escaped from Libby Prison in February
1864.

Lt. John Vliet, Age 29
Co. D, 84th New York
Survived.

Lt. William Wheeler
N.Y. Light Artillery, 13th Battery
Survived.

Maj. Edwin B. Wight, 24th Michigan
Shot in the eye and survived.

Pvt. Bradley F. Yates, Co. K, 20th North Carolina
Severely wounded in the right arm in Forney's Field
on Oak Ridge and captured on July 5. His arm
amputated; paroled in September 1863.

Albert H. (L) and Jonathan Clark, Co. F., 42nd Mississippi
Both killed on July 1, along with their father.

Thursday, July 2
Summary

As the fighting subsided on July 1, Lee and Lieutenant General James Longstreet considered their battle plans. They studied the Union position through their field glasses. Union Major General George G. Meade's subordinates had established a strong defensive position on Culp's Hill and Cemetery Hill and Ridge. Lee decided that if the Army of the Potomac (Union) remained at Gettysburg that he would attack on July 2.

Lee based his battle strategy on information that the Union line started near Culp's Hill and ended on Cemetery Ridge, somewhere near the modern Pennsylvania Monument. He proposed a three-pronged attack.

Longstreet's two divisions would lead the main thrust; they were ordered to secretly deploy on the right flank. Once in position they would strike up the Emmitsburg Road and roll up the Union left flank on Cemetery Ridge. Confederate Lieutenant General Ambrose P. Hill's Corps would strike the Union center on Cemetery Ridge and Cemetery Hill, essentially preventing reinforcements from being sent to either flank. Confederate Lieutenant General Richard Ewell's Corps, on the left flank, would attack the enemy's right, Culp's Hill and East Cemetery Hill, and, if opportunity offered, convert the demonstration into a real assault. Lee had on hand about 50,000 men and 200 guns.

Meade arrived in Gettysburg around 1:00 a.m., July 2. As his army arrived he positioned them on Culp's Hill, Cemetery Hill and Cemetery Ridge. Around 2:00 p.m. Major General Daniel Sickles redeployed his III Corps on the Emmitsburg Road, Peach Orchard, Wheatfield and Devil's Den. Meade counted around 70,000 soldiers and 350 cannon.

The Confederate infantry assault began between 4:00 and 4:30 p.m. The fighting raged around Little Round Top, Devil's Den, the Wheatfield, Peach Orchard until about 6:30 p.m. Sometime after 6:00 p.m., A.P. Hill's Corps hit the Union troops along the Emmitsburg Road. One Confederate unit, Brigadier General Ambrose Wright's Georgia brigade, breached the Cemetery Ridge line, just south of the Copse of Trees. Yet, without reinforcements the Georgians were forced to retreat. The fighting on the Union center ended around 7:30 p.m. As the battle ended in that region, Ewell's Confederate Corps attacked the Union right on Culp's Hill and East Cemetery Hill. The Confederates turned the Union right flank on Culp's Hill, but due to darkness they were unable to follow up on their success. On East Cemetery Hill two Confederate brigades broke through the line. Without reinforcements, out of ammunition, and exhausted, the Confederates withdrew.

The casualties estimated for the entire day were 7,800 Union and 7,300 Confederates.

Capt. Andrew Ackerman, Co. C, 11th New Jersey
Killed near the Emmitsburg Road.

Sgt. Franklin Adams, Co. K, 17th Maine
Wounded in the hand during the fight in the
Wheatfield.

Lt. Jerome Allen, Co. G, 4th Michigan
Survived the Wheatfield.

Pvt. Quintin Anderson, Co. H, 6th North Carolina
Charged up East Cemetery Hill; survived.

Lt. Daniel Banta, Co. I, 66th New York
Wounded in the Wheatfield; survived.

Sgt. Beverly Barksdale, Co. B, 22nd Georgia
Captured.

Pvt. Charles Barrett, Age 21
Co. G, 4th Michigan
Survived the Wheatfield.

Lt. William Benjamin, Co. G, 124th New York
Fought near Devil's Den;

Pvts. Eli (L) and Charles Bickmore
Cos. I and E, 20th Maine
Both survived.

Capt. Julius W. Boyd, Age 29, Co. H, 20th Georgia
Boyd's regiment assaulted Devil's Den and captured
three cannon. He survived.

Sgt. Ezra Brown, Co. K, 4th Michigan
Fought in the Wheatfield and escaped injury.

Capt. T. Fred Brown
1st Rhode Island Light Artillery, Battery B
Shot through the body, but survived.

Pvt. Thomas Burt (seated) and friend, J. Jenkins
Co. H, 62nd Pennsylvania
Fought in the Wheatfield and survived.

Pvt. John A. Byers, Co. H, 17th Mississippi
Wounded and captured.

Pvt. Elisha Coan, Co. F, 20th Maine
Wrote of the fight on Little Round Top, "...all I could
do is bight (sic) my lips..."

Sgt. David W. Colburn, Age 21
Co. C, 2nd New Hampshire
Shot in the head and killed.

Sgt. John Cooley, Age 32
Co. A, 28th Massachusetts
Mortally wounded in the Wheatfield, died July 3.

Lt. Joseph S. Coulter, Age 22
Co. D, 53rd Massachusetts
Survived the Wheatfield.

Lt. George T. Curvan, Co. F, 148th Pennsylvania
Wounded in the head, survived.

Lt. Horatio David, Co. B, 16th Georgia
Survived, wounded and blinded in 1864.

Lt. James DeGray, Co. G, 1st Minnesota
Severely wounded but survived.

Lt. Christopher Erickson, Age 27
9th Massachusetts Light Artillery, killed.

Lt. and Adjutant Henry Figures (L), 48th Alabama
Cited for Bravery; killed in the Wilderness, 1864.

Capt. Henry Fuller, Age 22, Co. F, 64th New York
Hit in the eye and killed in the Wheatfield.

Col. William Gibson, 48th Georgia
Shot through the thighs and captured.

Cpl. Nelson Gilbert, Co. I, 149th New York
On Culp's Hill, wounded in the left eye and head, but
survived.

Pvt. Francis M. Griswold, Co. C, 44th New York
Defending Little Round Top, shot in the head and
killed instantly. Buried in National Cemetery.

Lt. Charles M. Harper, Co. E, 8th Georgia
In Devil's Den, wounded but survived.

Pvt. Alonzo C. Hayden, Age 22
Co. D, 1st Minnesota, killed.

Cpl. Judson A. Hicks, Age 26, Co. A, 111th New York
Hit five times while carrying the colors, killed.

Pvt. George Henry "Hank" Hudson
Co. E, 86th New York
Fought in the Devil's Den and survived.

Capt. Rueben Vaughan Kidd, Co. A, 4th Alabama
Survived Little Round Top, killed at Chickamauga.

Pvt. Wesley Knott, Age 19, Co. A, 6th North Carolina
Survived, died in 1916.

Pvt. J. H. Lively, Co. K, 48th Alabama
Survived the Slaughter Pen.

Capt. Dorastus B. Logan, Co. H, 11th New Jersey
Killed near the Emmitsburg Road.

Pvt. Oren Lord, Co. K, 17th Maine
Survived the Wheatfield.

Capt. Thomas R. Love, Co. B, 8th Florida
Laid wounded on the field for three days, died.

Cpl. Michael Maloy, Age 23, Co. C, 57th Pennsylvania
Killed near the Peach Orchard.

Col. Van H. Manning, 3rd Arkansas, with his wife
Survived assault on Devil's Den.

Capt. Luther Martin, Co. D, 11th New Jersey
Shot and killed near the Emmitsburg Road.

Pvt. Adam Marty, Co. B, 1st Minnesota
Wounded but survived.

Lt. Henry D. McDaniel, Co. H, 11th Georgia
Survived Devil's Den, wounded
and captured, July 12.

Pvt. John McNutt, Co. G, 140th Pennsylvania
Killed in action near the Wheatfield.

Sgt. James McPherson
Co. C, 5th Pennsylvania Reserves
Survived, but brother killed on July 1st.

Capt. Richard S. Milton
9th Massachusetts Light Artillery
Fought near the Wheatfield and Trostle's Farm.

Pvt. Archibald G. Morrison, Age 23
Co. D, 2nd Florida
Wounded in left shoulder and knee, survived.

Pvt. Scott Munson, Co. F, 44th New York
Shot in the head and killed on Little Round Top.

Col. James Drayton Nance, 3rd South Carolina
Fought in the Wheatfield and survived.

Capt. Isaac Nicholl, Age 23, Co. G, 124th New York
Killed in the Devil's Den.

Capt. Matthew T. Nunnally, Age 24
Co. H, 11th Georgia
Fought in the Rose Woods, Wheatfield, killed.

Capt. James Patterson, Age 24
Co. G, 148th Pennsylvania
Dickinson College graduate, survived the Wheatfield.

Lt. Walter S. Perrin, 1st Rhode Island Light, Batt. B
Slightly wounded on July 3rd.

Sgt. Charles H. Phelps, Age 19
Co. I, 5th New Hampshire
Wounded in the Wheatfield, died on July 3rd.

Pvt. Isaac A. Reed, Co. H, 7th Georgia
Survived, shot three times in November 1863.

Pvt. Francis W. Rhoades, Age 26, Co. I, 19th Maine
Killed.

Pvt. John H. Roberts, Co. E, 5th Texas
Wounded in both legs, Union soldiers built a
protecting wall for him. Survived, captured.

Lt. Benjamin Franklin Rogers, Co. D, 2nd Georgia
Assumed command of regiment, survived.

Sgt. H. Shaffer, Co. F, 62nd Pennsylvania
Killed in the Wheatfield.

Sgt. Robert F. Shipley, Co. A, 44th New York
Survived, awarded Medal of Honor in 1865.

Pvt. Charles Speisberger, Age 18
Co. D, 140th New York
Killed on Little Round Top.

Pvt. John L. Stewart, Co. G, 48th Virginia
Fought on Culp's Hill, survived.

Pvt. Joseph DeWitt Stroud, Co. K, 13th Mississippi
Killed.

Cpls. Patrick (L) and Isaac Taylor
Co. I, 1st Minnesota
Isaac killed by an artillery shell, buried by Patrick.

Lt. Evan Thomas, 4th U.S. Artillery, Battery C
His battery helped repulse attacks on Cemetery Ridge
on July 2nd and 3rd, survived.

Pvt. Francis C. Tucker, Age 19
9th Massachusetts Light Artillery
Survived, died in 1929, buried in Arlington.

Pvt. Ira Thomas Turner, Co. G, 7th South Carolina
Wounded near the Wheatfield, survived.

Pvt. John Unger, Jr., Age 19
Co. K, 40th New York
Fought near Devil's Den, survived.

Cpl. Erastus Walters, Co. G, 4th Michigan
Fought in the Wheatfield; wounded, survived.

Col. George H. Ward, Age 37, 15th Massachusetts
Mortally wounded, died July 3rd.

Lt. Henry Clay Ward, 15th Massachusetts
Brother of Col. George Ward, survived.

Lt. Alexander H. Whitbaker, Age 20
9th Massachusetts Light Artillery
Mortally wounded, died July 20.

Lt. Daniel W. Williams, Co. I, 61st Ohio
Shot in the lungs on East Cemetery Hill,
died on July 5th.

Sgt. William T. Williams, Co. K, 114th Pennsylvania
Shot in the shoulder, survived.

Lt Jesse Bowman Young, Co. B, 84th Pennsylvania
Detached from 84th, acted as Asst. Provost Marshall,
later wrote a history of the battle.

Friday, July 3

Lee's strategy for July 3 was essentially an extension from his July 2 plan. This time, however, the Confederates' main thrust would come at the center of the Union line. Approximately 12,500 infantrymen from three divisions commanded by Major General George Pickett, Major General Isaac Trimble and Brigadier General J. J. Pettigrew would cross a mile-wide field and hit Cemetery Ridge near the Copse of Trees. At the same time Ewell's Corps would make a demonstration on Culp's Hill and continue threatening the Union right. As the infantrymen fought, Major General Jeb Stuart's cavalry would ride around the Union line and would attempt to strike at its rear.

The Union foiled the Confederate plan early on Friday morning. They preempted the assault on Culp's Hill. Ewell, therefore, committed his men and attacked in force. After five hours the assault ended as Union troops pushed the Confederates off the hill. Lee, nevertheless, determined to attack the infantry line on Cemetery Ridge. Around 1:00 p.m. a huge cannonade began. For two hours over 250 guns fired shot and shell; smoke engulfed the area. At 3:00 p.m. the Confederate infantrymen started their mile-long march. Union artillery wrecked havoc on their lines. By 3:20-3:30 p.m. the infantrymen hit the Union line. They broke through in several places, but without reinforcements they were unable to capitalize on their partial success. Union officers rushed regiments into the danger areas, and the Confederates were either killed, wounded, captured or retreated.

Casualties for July 3 numbered about 10,100 Americans. The bloody three-day casualty toll is around 40,000 killed and wounded, another 10,000 captured or missing.

Bugler Joe Allen, Co. I, 1st Vermont Cavalry
Survived Farnsworth's Charge. He left his wounded
horse behind, but it followed him 60 miles.

Capt. William A. Arnold, 1st Rhode Island, Batt. A
Aided in repulse of Pickett's Charge and survived.

Pvt. George D. Barnes, Age 19, Co. K, 9th Virginia
Wounded in the knee in front of the stone wall during
Pickett's Charge, captured.

Cpl. Jacob L. Bechtel, Co. B, 59th New York
Defended Cemetery Ridge on July 2nd and 3rd,
survived.

Pvt. Jacob Bowen(L), 18th Maine, with son
Pvt. John Bowen, 1st Maine Cavalry
Jacob not at Gettysburg, John survived.

Major James Kaell Burns, 5th North Carolina Cavalry
Killed.

Pvt. Charles Camm, 1st Richmond Howitzers
Survived.

Pvt. William G. Cason, Co. H, 57th Virginia
Mortally wounded in Pickett's Charge.

Sgt. Charles S. Chichester, Age 20
Co. A, 150th New York
Fought on Culp's Hill, survived.

Sgt.. Darius Cliborne, Co. F, 14th Virginia
Captured during Pickett's Charge.

Pvt. James M. Coleman, Co. H, 24th Virginia
Killed in action during Pickett's Charge.

Pvt. Henry Couillon, Co. A, 40th New York
Hit in the spine and killed.

Pvt. John Wesley Culp, Age 24, Co. B, 2nd Virginia
Former Gettysburg resident, killed on July 3rd on his
cousin's farm near Culp's Hill.

Capt. Ignatius W. Dorsey, Co. A, 1st Maryland
Battalion Cavalry, C.S.A. On Lt. Gen. Richard
Ewell's staff. Survived.

Pvt. Sanford Bertram Duff
Co. H, 57th Virginia
Survived Pickett's Charge.

Pvt. Joseph Kent Ewing, Co. G, 4th Virginia
Killed on Culp's Hill.

Capt. Thomas B. Fox, Age 24
Co. K, 2nd Massachusetts
Mortally wounded in Spangler's Meadow.

Sgt. Thomas Geer, Age 23, Co. A, 111th New York
Wrote "my gun was shot all to pieces before I could fire
a shot, it tore my coat sleeve and bruised my arm."

Pvt. Charles Graves, Co. G, 16th Vermont
Survived repulse of Pickett's Charge.

Orderly Sgt. Caleb Griffith
Co. C, 7th Michigan Cavalry
Wounded in the head, survived.

Pvt. John Haverstick, Age 17
Co. I, 12th New Jersey
Suffered heat stroke; survived.

Capt. Jonathan Hankins, Co. C, 16th Virginia Cavalry
Commanded four brothers and his father in his
company. Survived.

Sgt. Samuel Holland, Co. E, 9th Virginia
Wounded in Pickett's Charge; survived.

Sgt. Reuben Howerter, Age 21
Co. H, 147th Pennsylvania
Shot through the heart on Culp's Hill.

Sgt. John Ibaugh, Co. E, 29th Pennsylvania
Fought on Culp's Hill, survived.

Sgt. William N. Irving, Co. D, 1st Minnesota
Color-bearer, survived.

Pvt. Benjamin Jenkinson
Co. A, 3rd Pennsylvania Cavalry
Survived.

Pvt. Carroll Charles Kirchner, Age 24
Co. C, 4th Pennsylvania Cavalry
Survived.

Pvt. Benjamin Lewis Lanham
Co. C, 1st Battalion Maryland Infantry, C.S.A.
Killed in action on Culp's Hill.

Sgt. Michael Lawn, Co. K, 95th Pennsylvania
Survived.

Sgt. Joseph W. Lehr
Co. M, 16th Pennsylvania Cavalry
Survived.

Pvt. Benjamin F. Lincoln
Co. G, 10th Virginia Cavalry
Abraham Lincoln's cousin. Survived.

Pvt. David D. Liptrap, Co. K, 52nd Virginia
Wounded in shoulder in Pickett's Charge, survived.

Sgt. Conrad Mehne, Co. K, 27th Indiana
Killed in Spangler's Meadow near Culp's Hill.

Cpl. Thomas Jefferson Melton
Fluvanna (Virginia) Artillery
Survived.

Pvt. Lucas Lewis Meredith, Co. C, 3rd Virginia
Color-bearer in Pickett's Charge, survived.

Pvt. John Henry Miles, Co. C, 57th Virginia
Survived Pickett's Charge.

Pvt. Lindith Mitchell, Age 22
Co. G, 28th Virginia
Survived Pickett's Charge.

Pvt. Robert James Morris, Co. H, 57th Virginia
Survived Pickett's Charge.

Sgt. John M. Nash, Co. G, 1st Vermont Cavalry
Survived Farnsworth's Charge.

Pvt. Caleb (L) and Cpl. Jeremiah Nead
Co. M, 16th Pennsylvania Cavalry
Both father and son survived the battle.

Capt. Chancellor A. Nelson, Co. B, 49th Virginia
Wounded and captured during skirmish, July 5th.

Pvt. George D. Nethery, Age 29, Co. G, 14th Virginia
Marching near Armistead, he was wounded in the
shoulder but returned to the lines.

Lt. J. D. Newson, Co. I, 47th North Carolina
Wounded in the shoulder and foot near Emmitsburg
Road during Pickett's Charge, he survived.

Capt. James K. O'Reilly, Co. E, 8th Ohio
Helped repulse Pickett's Charge and survived.

Capt. Henry T. Owen, Age 32, Co. C, 18th Virginia
At the end of Pickett's Charge he commanded his
regiment.

Lt. Sumner Paine, Age 18, Co. A, 20th Massachusetts
Killed by a shell fragment during the cannonade.

Pvt. John Paris, Co. D, 1st Delaware
Captured near Bliss barn.

Capt. Charles A. Phillips, Age 21
5th Massachusetts Battery
Fought near the Wheatfield, survived.

Pvt. Joseph Pierce, Co. F, 14th Connecticut
Only soldier of Chinese descent in the Army of the
Potomac; survived.

Lt. William H. Pohlman, Age 22, Adj., 59th New York
Wounded in left shoulder during cannonade, in the
wrist in Pickett's Charge; died July 21.

Bugler John Robinson
Co. D, 4th Pennsylvania Cavalry
Survived.

Pvt. Marshall Sherman, Co. C, 1st Minnesota
Captured flag of 28th Virginia in the Angle.

Lt. H.V.D. Stone, 2nd Massachusetts, Age 19
Shot in the head in Spangler's Meadow, killed.

Pvt. Charles Strewing, Co. H, 42nd New York
Enlisted at 17, was 18 during battle; survived.

Col. William Dabney Stuart, 56th Virginia
Killed during Pickett's Charge.

Cpl. George Stuart, Co. G, 72nd Pennsylvania
Killed.

Sgt. John Stuart, Age 32, Co. G, 72nd Pennsylvania
Brother of George; survived.

Cpl. Londus F. Terrill, Co. F, 13th Vermont
Claimed to have shot Gen. James Kemper; survived.

Capt. Samuel P. Wagg, Co. A, 26th North Carolina
Shot through the body with shrapnel, killed.

Pvts. Howard M. (L, Co. D), 1st Virginia, and Robert "Ryland" Walthall, Co. G, 1st Virginia. Howard survived, Robert was killed at Drewry's Bluff in 1864.

Capt. John C. Ward, Age 31, Co. E, 11th Virginia Captured.

Sgt. J. A. Whitley (survived), Capt. E. Fletcher Satterfield (killed), Sgt. T.D. Falls (survived), 55th North Carolina, claimed furthest advance during Pickett's Charge.

Pvt. James Wilson, Co. G, 14th Virginia
Survived Pickett's Charge, mortally wounded at
Bermuda Hundred, July, 1864.

Dr. Frederick A. Dudley, 14th Connecticut
Wounded in the arm by a shell fragment, survived.

Dr. Justin Dwinelle, 106th Pennsylvania
Survived.

Dr. E. LeBaron Monroe, 15th Massachusetts
Survived.

Dr. Thomas Palmer, 2nd Florida
Survived.

Photo-Bibliography

GNMP: Gettysburg National Military Park
USAMHI: United States Military History Institute, Photo archives, Carlisle, Pennsylvania.
    Clark: Walter Clark, ed., Histories of the Several Regiments and Battalions from North Carolina in the Great War, 1861-1865
5 Vols. (Raleigh: State of North Carolina, 1901.

* * * * *

July 1

1. Pvt. M. Hezekiah Allen, Ms. Kim Cupples Coll. via GNMP
2. Pvt. George H. Atkins, USAMHI
3. Capt. G.T. Baskerville, Clark, Vol. 2
4. Pvt. Charles E. Beard, Mr. Lance C. Arlander Coll. via GNMP
5. Pvt. Phillip Bennetts, Mr. Kenneth Sedbrook Coll. via GNMP
6. Pvt. Peter Boyer, Mr. Clayton Boyer Coll. via GNMP
7. Pvt. George Brodmerkel, Mr. Jeffrey Anderson Coll. via GNMP
8. Cpl. James Brown, Mr. Jeff Kowalis Coll. via GNMP
9. Col. H.K. Burgwyn, Clark, Vol 2
10. Lt. John Calef, USAMHI
11. Pvt. Chester Cammer, Mr. Carl G. Miller Coll. via GNMP
12. 2d Lt. Benjamin F. Carr, Maine State Archives Coll. via GNMP
13. Pvts. Albert and Jonathan Clark, USAMHI
14. Sgt. Jefferson Coates, USAMHI
15. Pvt. William H. Connell, Mr. Robert G. Connell Coll. via GNMP
16. Pvt. Charles Cosgrave, Mr. Edward J. Cosgrove Coll. via GNMP
17. Maj. Edward Croft, Citadel Coll. via GNMP
18. Capt. Simeon B. David, Mr. W. Miller Logan, M.D. Coll. via GNMP
19. Pvt. Frank H. Elvidge, Mr. Dale S. Snair Coll. via GNMP
20. Lt. J.R. Emerson, Mr. Don Scoggins Coll. via GNMP
21. Pvt. Edwin Field, Mr. Scott Hann Coll. via GNMP
22. Pvt. Joseph Frederick Haas, Mr. David K. Steindel Coll. via GNMP
23. Capt. James A. Hall, Maine State Archives Coll. via GNMP
24. Cpl. Franklin N. Halsey, GNMP Coll.
25. Pvt. John T. Handy, Ms. Judy Hudspeth Coll. via GNMP
26. Lt. William Harris, Ms. Pamela Harris Dennison Coll. via GNMP
27. Pvt. Jacob Harshberger, Mr. Thomas Harshberger Coll. via GNMP
28. Sgt. Amos Humiston, USAMHI
29. Pvt. William and Sgt. Charles Issermoyer, Lehigh County Historical Society Coll. via GNMP
30. Capt. Jacob Jacobs, USAMHI
31. Pvt. Alex Lameraux, Mr. Rod Berlin Coll. via GNMP
32. Pvt. Charles E. Leland, Mr. Scott Hann Coll. via GNMP
33. Pvt. Michael McGurren, Mr. Michael Winkelman Coll. via GNMP
34. Cpl. Benjamin McPherson, Mr. Scott Hann Coll. via GNMP
35. Capt. Daniel Marston, Maine States Archives Coll. via GNMP
36. Cpl. James Martindale, Mr. John F. Macon Coll. via GNMP
37. Cpl. Henry A. Miller, Ms. Lucy Storch Coll. via GNMP
38. Pvt. John Moy, Mr. Richard Moy Coll. via GNMP
39. Pvt. Isaac P. Nichols, USAMHI via GNMP
40. Pvt. George F. Newton, Mr. Jeffrey Grable Coll. via GNMP
41. Sgt. Robert Niven, USAMHI via GNMP
42. Pvt. Valentine Painter, Mr. Bruce Hoffman Coll. via GNMP
43. 2d Sgt. John H. Peifer, Mr. Norm Reigle Coll. via GNMP
44. Pvt. William H. Porter, Mr. Harry L. Porter Coll. via GNMP
45. Capt. John D.H. Robinson, Mr. John Britt Coll. via GNMP

46. Pvt. Jeremiah Royer, Mr. George A. Conte, Jr. Coll. via GNMP
47. Col. William Sackett, USAMHI via GNMP
48. Pvt. Thomas Coates Sheppard, USAMHI
49. Lt. John J. Smith, USAMHI via GNMP
50. Pvt. William Franklin Smith, Ms. Catherine Smith Coll. via USAMHI
51. Pvt. Edward Sonneberg, Mr. Ray Fuerschbach Coll. via GNMP
52. Pvt. Benjamin L. Taylor, Mr. Jeff Stepp Coll. via GNMP
53. 1st Lt. John Fred Tinker, USAMHI via GNMP
54. Lt. Morton Tower, Mr. Scott Hann Coll. via GNMP
55. Lt. John Vliet, USAMHI via GNMP
56. Lt. William Wheeler, USAMHI
57. Maj. Edwin B. Wight, Mr. Scott Hann Coll. via GNMP
58. Pvt. Bradley F. Yates, Mr. Richard W. Bullock Coll. via GNMP

July 2

1. Capt. Andrew H. Ackerman, Mr. John Kuhl Coll. via GNMP
2. Sgt. Franklin C. Adams, Maine State Archives Coll. via GNMP
3. 1st Lt. Jerome Allen, Mr. Richard Betterly Coll. via GNMP
4. Pvt. Quintin T. Anderson, Mr. Ken Anderson Coll. via GNMP
5. Lt. Daniel Banta, USAMHI via GNMP
6. Sgt. Beverly E. Barksdale, Mr. W. Miller Logan, M.D. Coll. via GNMP
7. Pvt. Charles H. Barrett, Mr. Richard Betterly Coll. via GNMP
8. Lt. William H. Benjamin, USAMHI via GNMP
9. Pvts. Eli and Charles Bickmore, Glenn Coll. via GNMP
10. Capt. Julius W. Boyd, Mr. Keith Bohannon Coll. via GNMP
11. Sgt. Ezra Brown, Mr. Roger Davis Coll. via GNMP
12. Capt. T. Fred Brown, Thomas Aldrich, History of Battery A
13. Pvt. Thomas Burt, Mr. Stanley A. Burt Coll. via GNMP
14. Pvt. John A. Byers, Ms. Mary Ann Rogers Coll. via GNMP
15. Pvt. Elisha Coan, Bowdoin College Archives Coll. via GNMP
16. 1st Sgt. David W. Colburn, Mr. Jeff Kowalis Coll. via GNMP
17. Sgt. John Cooley, Ms. Catherine Cooley Fay Coll. via GNMP
18. 2d Lt. Joseph S. Coulter, Mr. Edward W. Wade Coll. via GNMP
19. 2d Lt. George T. Curvan, Mr. Gordon C. Curvan Coll. via GNMP
20. 2d Lt. Horatio J. David, Mr. W. Miller Logan, M.D. Coll. via GNMP
21. 2d Lt. James DeGray, Minnesota Historical Society Coll. via GNMP
22. 1st Lt. Christopher Erickson, Mr. Edmund T. Girard Coll. via GNMP
23. Lt. Henry Figures, Mr. John Pannick Coll. via GNMP
24. Capt. Henry Fuller, Mr. Orton Begner Coll. via GNMP
25. Col. William Gibson, Mr. George H. Shands Coll. via GNMP
26. Cpl. Nelson Gilbert, USAMHI via GNMP
27. Pvt. Francis M. Griswold, Mr. Charles Zukowski Coll. via GNMP
28. 1st Lt. Charles M. Harper, Mr. Keith Bohannon Coll. via GNMP
29. Pvt. Alonzo C. Hayden, Mr. Stephen Bartel Coll. via GNMP
30. Cpl. Judson A. Hicks, Mr. David B. Crane Coll. via GNMP
31. Pvt. George H. Hudson, Mr. Kurt Holman Coll. via GNMP
32. Capt. Reuben V. Kidd, Mr. Dale S. Snair Coll. via GNMP
33. Pvt. Wesley Knott, Mr. Richard Zigler Coll. via GNMP
34. Pvt. J.H. Lively, Elsie Connell Coll. via GNMP
35. Capt. Dorastus B. Logan, Mr. John Kuhl Coll. via GNMP
36. Pvt. Oren Lord, Mr. Harvey Lord Coll. via GNMP
37. Capt. Thomas R. Love, Mr. Robert Baldwin Coll. via GNMP
38. Cpl. Michael Maloy, Mr. Arthur O'Leary Coll. via GNMP
39. Col. Van H. Manning and wife, University of Arkansas Coll. via USAMHI
40. Capt. Luther Martin, Mr. John Kuhl Coll. via GNMP
41. Pvt. Adam Marty, Minnesota Historical Society Coll. via GNMP
42. Lt. Henry D. McDaniel, Mr. Keith Bohannon Coll. via GNMP

43. Pvt. John McNutt, Mr. George W. Neely Coll. via GNMP
44. Sgt. James McPherson, Mr. Scott Hann Coll. via GNMP
45. Capt. Richard S. Milton, USAMHI
46. Pvt. Archibald G. Morrison, Mr. Robert Baldwin Coll. via GNMP
47. Pvt. Scott Munson, USAMHI via GNMP
48. Col. James Drayton Nance, Citadel Coll. via GNMP
49. Capt. Isaac Nicoll, USAMHI via GNMP
50. Capt. Matthew Talbot Nunnally, Mr. Keith Bohannon Coll. via GNMP
51. Capt. James Patterson, History of the 148th Pennsylvania via GNMP
52. Lt. Walter S. Perrin, Thomas Aldrich, History of Battery A
53. Sgt. Charles H. Phelps, Mr. Steven C. Sexton Coll. via GNMP
54. Pvt. Isaac A. Reed, Mr. Keith Bohannon Coll. via GNMP
55. Pvt. Francis W. Rhoades, GNMP Coll.
56. Pvt. John H. Roberts, Mr. John L. Roberts Coll. via GNMP
57. 2d Lt. Benjamin Franklin Rogers, Mr. Ben C. Rogers Coll. via GNMP
58. Sgt. William H. Shaffer, Mr. William Shaffer, Jr. Coll. via GNMP
59. Sgt. Robert F. Shipley, USAMHI via GNMP
60. Pvt. Charles Speisberger, Ms. Carolyn Sickelco Coll. via GNMP
61. Pvt. John L. Stewart, Stewart Family Coll. via GNMP
62. Pvt. Joseph DeWitt Stroud, LTC. James L. Quinnelly, Ret. Coll. via GNMP
63. Cpls. Patrick (L) and Isaac (R) Taylor, Minnesota Historical Society Coll. via GNMP
64. Lt. Evan Thomas, USAMHI
65. Pvt. Francis C. Tucker, Ms. Lynn Nichols Coll. via GNMP
66. Pvt. Ira Thomas Turner, Mrs. Turner Greenwald Coll. via GNMP
67. Cpl. Erastus Walters, Mr. Richard Betterly Coll. via GNMP
68. Col. George H. Ward, USAHMI
69. 2d Lt. Henry C. Ward, Mr. George M. Aldenbourgh Coll. via GNMP
70. 1st Lt. Alexander H. Whitbaker, USAMHI
71. 2d Lt. Daniel W. Williams, Ms. Linda Gallagher Coll. via GNMP
72. Sgt. William T. Williams, Mr. John B. Sidebotham Coll. via GNMP
73. Pvt. John Unger, Jr., GNMP Coll.
74. Lt. Jesse Bowman Young, May Morris Room Coll., Dickinson College

July 3

1. Bugler Joe Allen, Mr. George A. Hughs Coll. via GNMP
2. Capt. William A. Arnold, USAMHI
3. Pvt. George D. Barnes, Mr. Tilden F. Barnes, Jr. Coll. via GNMP
4. Cpl. Jacob L. Bechtel, GNMP
5. Pvts. Jacob and John Bowen, Paul and Margie Bowen Coll. via GNMP
6. Maj. James Kaell Burns, Citadel Coll. via GNMP
7. Pvt. Charles Camm, Mr. Dale S. Snair Coll. via GNMP
8. Pvt. William G. Cason, Mr. Carl M. Cason Coll. via GNMP
9. Sgt. Charles S. Chichester, USAMHI via GNMP
10. Sgt. Darius Cliborne, Ms. Barbara Buchanan Coll. via GNMP
11. Pvt. James M. Coleman, Mrs. Galileo S. Clark
12. Pvt. Henri Couillon, Ms. Dorothy Leslie Coll. via GNMP
13. Pvt. John Wesley Culp, GNMP Coll.
14. Capt. Ignatius W. Dorsey, Mr. John S. Mattson Coll. via GNMP
15. Pvt. Sanford Bertram Duff, Ms. Eva Shillingburg Coll. via GNMP
16. Pvt. Joseph Kent Ewing, Mr. Herb Peck, Jr. Coll. via GNMP
17. Capt. Thomas B. Fox, USAMHI
18. Sgt. Thomas Geer, Mr. David Crane Coll. via GNMP
19. Pvt. Charles Graves, Mr. Charles Graves Coll. via GNMP
20. Ord. Sgt. Caleb Griffith, Mr. Richard L. Frink Coll. via GNMP
21. 1st Sgt. Reuben A. Howerter, Mr. W.F. Steigerwalt Coll. via GNMP
22. Pvt. John Haverstick, GNMP Coll.
23. Capt. Jonathan Hankins, Mr. Thomas Hankins Coll. via GNMP

24. Sgt. Samuel Hardy Holland, Mr. Robert E. Holland Coll. via GNMP
25. Sgt. John Ibaugh, GNMP
26. Cpl. William Irving, Minnesota Historical Society Coll. via GNMP
27. Pvt. Benjamin Jenkinson, Florence Fahs Coll. via GNMP
28. Pvt. Carroll Charles Kirchner, Mr. James E. Ashbaugh Coll. via GNMP
29. Pvt. Benjamin Lewis Lanham, Dr. Howard Lanham Coll. via USAMHI
30. Sgt. Michael Lawn, USAMHI via GNMP
31. Sgt. Joseph W. Lehr, Mrs. Rosemary Johnson Coll. via GNMP
32. Pvt. Benjamin F. Lincoln, Mr. Dale S. Snair Coll. via GNMP
33. Pvt. David D. Liptrap, Mr. Dale S. Snair Coll. via GNMP
34. Sgt. Conrad Mehne, Mr. James L. Mehn Coll. via GNMP
35. Cpl. Thomas Jefferson Melton, Mr. Dale S. Snair Coll. via GNMP
36. Pvt. Lucas Lewis Meredith, Meredith Family Coll. via GNMP
37. Pvt. John Henry Miles, Mr. Michael M. Meador Coll. via GNMP
38. Pvt. Lindith Mitchell, Mr. Frank R. Chrzanowski Coll. via GNMP
39. Pvt. Robert James Morris, Ms. Linda Gittoes (Morris) Coll. via GNMP
40. Sgt. John M. Nash, St. Albans Historical Society Coll. via GNMP
41. Pvt. Caleb (L) and Jeremiah (R) Nead, Mr. Rodney J. Angle Coll. via GNMP
42. Capt. Chancellor A. Nelson, Mr. Dale S. Snair Coll. via GNMP
43. Pvt. George D. Nethery, Mr. J. Marshall Neathery Coll. via GNMP
44. 2d Lt. J.D. Newson, Clark
45. Capt. James K. O'Reilly, Mr. Kenneth Callahan Coll. via GNMP
46. Capt. Henry T. Owen, F.A. Yates Coll. via GNMP
47. Pvt. John Paris, Mr. Richard J. Vernon Coll. via GNMP
48. Lt. Sumner Paine, USAMHI
49. Pvt. Joseph Pierce, Charles Page, History of the 14th Connecticut.
50. Lt. William H. Pohlman, USAMHI via GNMP
51. Capt. Charles A. Phillips, USAMHI
52. Bugler John G. Robinson, Mr. Rex Robinson McHail, Jr. Coll. via GNMP
53. Lt. H.V.D. Stone, USAMHI
54. Pvt. Charles Strewing, Mr. Bob Coch Coll. via GNMP
55. Pvt. Marshall Sherman, Minnesota Historical Society Coll. via GNMP
56. Cpl. George Stuart, Mr. Michael Christine Coll. via GNMP
57. Sgt. John Stuart, Mr. Michael Christine Coll. via GNMP
58. Col. William Dabney Stuart, Mr. Scott Hann Coll. via GNMP
59. Cpl. Londus F. Terrill, History of the 13th Vermont
60. Capt. Samuel P. Wagg, Clark
61. Pvts. Howard (L) and Robert (R) "Ryland" Walthall, Ms. Grace Walthall Turner Karish Coll. via GNMP
62. Capt. John C. Ward, Mr. Paul Smith Coll. via GNMP
63. J.A. Whitley, Capt. E. Fletcher Satterfield, T.D. Falls, Clark
64. Pvt. James Wilson, Mr. Michael A. Massaro Coll. via GNMP

Surgeons:

1. Dr. Frederick A. Dudley, Mr. Scott Hann Coll. via GNMP
2. Dr. Justin Dwinelle, Mr. Scott Dwinelle Coll. via GNMP
3. Dr. E. LeBaron Monroe, USAMHI
4. Dr. Thomas Palmer, Florida State Archives Coll. via USAMHI